THE
SEVEN
SPIRITUAL
LAWS
OF
SUCCESS

THE
SEVEN
SPIRITUAL
LAWS
OF
SUCCESS

A PRACTICAL GUIDE
TO THE FULFILLMENT
of YOUR DREAMS

DEEPAK CHOPRA

 AMBER-ALLEN PUBLISHING

 NEW WORLD LIBRARY

Based on the book *Creating Affluence: Wealth Consciousness in the Field of All Possibilities* © 1993 by Deepak Chopra

Co-published by Amber-Allen Publishing and New World Library

EDITORIAL OFFICE:
Amber-Allen Publishing
P.O. Box 6657
San Rafael, CA 94903

DISTRIBUTION OFFICE:
New World Library
58 Paul Drive
San Rafael, CA 94903

Editorial and production: Janet Mills
Type design and typography: Stephanie Eichleay
Cover design: Greg Wittrock, New York City
Cover art: Detail from *Asavari Ragini*, Subimperial Mughal, c. 1625

Library of Congress Cataloging-in-Publication Data
Chopra, Deepak.
     The seven spiritual laws of success : a practical guide to the fulfillment of your dreams / Deepak Chopra.
        p. cm.   "Based on the bestselling book, Creating affluence."
ISBN 1-878424-11-4 (alk. paper) : $12.95
1. Success in business—Religious aspects. 2. Success—Religious aspects. 3. Wealth—Psychological aspects. I. Chopra, Deepak. Creating affluence. II. Title.
HF5386.C5475 1994   94-35229
650.1—dc20   CIP

ISBN 1-878424-11-4
Printed in the U.S.A. on acid-free paper
Distributed by Publishers Group West

10 9 8 7 6

You are what your deep, driving desire is.

As your desire is, so is your will.

As your will is, so is your deed.

As your deed is, so is your destiny.

— *Brihadaranyaka Upanishad IV.4.5*

CONTENTS

ACKNOWLEDGMENTS

I would like to express my love and gratitude to the following people:

Janet Mills for lovingly nurturing this book from conception to completion.

Rita Chopra, Mallika Chopra, and Gautama Chopra for being the living expression of The Seven Spiritual Laws.

Ray Chambers, Gayle Rose, Adrianna Nienow, David Simon, George Harrison, Olivia Harrison, and Naomi Judd for their courage and commitment to a vision that is awesome, inspiring, lofty, noble, and life-transforming.

Roger Gabriel, Brent Becvar, Rose Bueno-Murphy, and all my staff at the Sharp Center for Mind-

Body Medicine for being inspiring examples to all our guests and patients.

Deepak Singh, Geeta Singh, and all my staff at Quantum Publications for their unflagging energy and dedication.

Muriel Nellis for her unflinching intention to maintain the highest level of integrity in all our endeavors.

Richard Perl for being such a great example of self-referral.

Linda Ford for her unshakable faith in self-knowledge and her infectious enthusiasm and commitment to transform the lives of so many people.

And Bill Elkus for his understanding and friendship.

INTRODUCTION

Although this book is titled *The Seven Spiritual Laws of Success*, it could also be called *The Seven Spiritual Laws of Life*, because these are the same principles that nature uses to create everything in material existence — everything we can see, hear, smell, taste, or touch.

In my book, *Creating Affluence: Wealth Consciousness in the Field of All Possibilities*, I have outlined the steps to wealth consciousness based on a true understanding of the workings of nature. *The Seven Spiritual Laws of Success* form the essence of this teaching. When this knowledge is incorporated in your consciousness, it will give you the ability to create unlimited wealth with effortless ease, and to experience success in every endeavor.

Success in life could be defined as the continued expansion of happiness and the progressive realization of worthy goals. Success is the ability to fulfill your desires with effortless ease. And yet success, including the creation of wealth, has always been considered to be a process that requires hard work, and it is often considered to be at the expense of others. We need a more spiritual approach to success and to affluence, which is the abundant flow of all good things to you. With the knowledge and practice of spiritual law, we put ourselves in harmony with nature and create with carefreeness, joy, and love.

There are many aspects to success; material wealth is only one component. Moreover, success is a journey, not a destination. Material abundance, in all its expressions, happens to be one of those things that makes the journey more enjoyable. But success also includes good health, energy and enthusiasm for life, fulfilling relationships, creative freedom, emotional and psychological stability, a sense of well-being, and peace of mind.

Even with the experience of all these things, we
will remain unfulfilled unless we nurture the seeds of
divinity inside us. In reality, we are divinity in disguise, and the gods and goddesses in embryo that are
contained within us seek to be fully materialized.
True success is therefore the experience of the miraculous. It is the unfolding of the divinity within us. It
is the perception of divinity wherever we go, in
whatever we perceive — in the eyes of a child, in the
beauty of a flower, in the flight of a bird. When we
begin to experience our life as the miraculous expression of divinity — not occasionally, but all the time
— then we will know the true meaning of success.

Before defining the seven spiritual laws, let us
understand the concept of law. Law is the process by
which the unmanifest becomes the manifest; it's the
process by which the observer becomes the observed;
it's the process by which the seer becomes the

scenery; it's the process through which the dreamer manifests the dream.

All of creation, everything that exists in the physical world, is the result of the unmanifest transforming itself into the manifest. Everything that we behold comes from the unknown. Our physical body, the physical universe — anything and everything that we can perceive through our senses — is the transformation of the unmanifest, unknown, and invisible into the manifest, known, and visible.

The physical universe is nothing other than the Self curving back within Itself to experience Itself as spirit, mind, and physical matter. In other words, all processes of creation are processes through which the Self or divinity expresses Itself. Consciousness in motion expresses itself as the objects of the universe in the eternal dance of life.

The source of all creation is divinity (or the spirit); the process of creation is divinity in motion (or the mind); and the object of creation is the physical universe (which includes the physical body).

These three components of reality — spirit, mind, and body, or observer, the process of observing, and the observed — are essentially the same thing. They all come from the same place: the field of pure potentiality which is purely unmanifest.

The physical laws of the universe are actually this whole process of divinity in motion, or consciousness in motion. When we understand these laws and apply them in our lives, anything we want can be created, because the same laws that nature uses to create a forest, or a galaxy, or a star, or a human body can also bring about the fulfillment of our deepest desires.

Now let's go over *The Seven Spiritual Laws of Success* and see how we can apply them in our lives.

∞ 1 ∞

THE LAW
OF PURE POTENTIALITY

*The source of all creation is pure
consciousness . . . pure potentiality seeking
expression from the unmanifest to the manifest.*

*And when we realize that our true Self is one
of pure potentiality, we align with the power
that manifests everything in the universe.*

In the beginning
There was neither existence nor non-existence,
All this world was unmanifest energy . . .

The One breathed, without breath, by Its own power
Nothing else was there . . .
— *Hymn of Creation, The Rig Veda*

The first spiritual law of success is the *Law of Pure Potentiality*. This law is based on the fact that we are, in our essential state, pure consciousness. Pure consciousness is pure potentiality; it is the field of all possibilities and infinite creativity. Pure consciousness is our spiritual essence. Being infinite and unbounded, it is also pure joy. Other attributes of consciousness are pure knowledge, infinite silence, perfect balance, invincibility, simplicity, and bliss. This is our essential nature. Our essential nature is one of pure potentiality.

When you discover your essential nature and know who you really are, *in that knowing itself* is the ability to fulfill any dream you have, because you are the eternal possibility, the immeasurable potential of all that was, is, and will be. The *Law of Pure Potentiality* could also be called the *Law of Unity*, because underlying the infinite diversity of life is the *unity* of one all-pervasive spirit. There is no separation between you and this field of energy. The field of pure potentiality is your own Self. And the more you experience your true nature, the closer you are to the field of pure potentiality.

The experience of the Self, or "self-referral," means that our internal reference point is our own spirit, and not the objects of our experience. The opposite of self-referral is object-referral. In object-referral we are always influenced by objects outside the Self, which include situations, circumstances, people, and things. In object-referral we are constantly seeking the approval of others. Our thinking and our behavior are always in anticipation of a response. It is therefore fear-based.

In object-referral we also feel an intense need to control things. We feel an intense need for external power. The need for approval, the need to control things, and the need for external power are needs that are based on fear. This kind of power is not the power of pure potentiality, or the power of the Self, or *real* power. When we experience the power of the Self, there is an absence of fear, there is no compulsion to control, and no struggle for approval or external power.

In object-referral, your internal reference point is your ego. The ego, however, is not who you really are. The ego is your self-image; it is your social mask; it is the role you are playing. Your social mask thrives on approval. It wants to control, and it is sustained by power, because it lives in fear.

Your true Self, which is your spirit, your soul, is completely free of those things. It is immune to criticism, it is unfearful of any challenge, and it feels beneath no one. And yet, it is also humble and feels superior to no one, because it recognizes that everyone else is the same Self, the same spirit in different disguises.

That's the essential difference between object-referral and self-referral. In self-referral, you experience your true being, which is unfearful of any challenge, has respect for all people, and feels beneath no one. Self-power is therefore true power.

Power based on object-referral, however, is false power. Being ego-based power, it lasts only as long as the object of reference is there. If you have a certain title — if you're the president of the country or the chairman of a corporation — or if you have a lot of money, the power you enjoy goes with the title, with the job, with the money. Ego-based power will only last as long as those things last. As soon as the title, the job, the money go away, so does the power.

Self-power, on the other hand, is permanent, because it is based on the knowledge of the Self. And there are certain characteristics of self-power.

It draws people to you, and it also draws things that you want to you. It magnetizes people, situations, and circumstances to support your desires. This is also called support from the laws of nature. It is the support of divinity; it is the support that comes from being in the state of grace. Your power is such that you enjoy a bond with people, and people enjoy a bond with you. Your power is that of bonding — a bonding that comes from true love.

How can we apply the *Law of Pure Potentiality*, the field of all possibilities, to our lives? If you want to enjoy the benefits of the field of pure potentiality, if you want to make full use of the creativity which is inherent in pure consciousness, then you have to have access to it. One way to access the field is through the daily practice of silence, meditation, and non-judgment. Spending time in nature will also give you access to the qualities inherent in the field: infinite creativity, freedom, and bliss.

Practicing silence means making a commitment to take a certain amount of time to simply *Be*. Experiencing silence means periodically withdrawing from the activity of speech. It also means periodically withdrawing from such activities as watching television, listening to the radio, or reading a book. If you never give yourself the opportunity to experience silence, this creates turbulence in your internal dialogue.

Set aside a little time every once in a while to experience silence. Or simply make a commitment to maintain silence for a certain period each day. You could do it for two hours, or if that seems a lot, do it for a one-hour period. And every once in a while experience silence for an extended period of time, such as a full day, or two days, or even a whole week.

What happens when you go into this experience of silence? Initially your internal dialogue becomes even more turbulent. You feel an intense need to say things. I've known people who go absolutely crazy the first day or two when they commit themselves to an extended period of silence. A sense of urgency and anxiety suddenly comes over them. But as they stay with the experience, their internal dialogue begins to quieten. And soon the silence becomes profound. This is because after a while the mind gives up; it realizes there is no point in going around and around if *you* — the Self, the spirit, the choice-maker — are not going to speak, period. Then, as the internal dialogue quietens, you begin to experience the stillness of the field of pure potentiality.

Practicing silence periodically as it is convenient to you is one way to experience the *Law of Pure Potentiality*. Spending time each day in meditation is another. Ideally, you should meditate at least thirty minutes in the morning, and thirty minutes in the evening. Through meditation you will learn to experience the field of pure silence and pure awareness. In that field of pure silence is the field of infinite correlation, the field of infinite organizing power, the ultimate ground of creation where everything is inseparably connected with everything else.

In the fifth spiritual law, the *Law of Intention and Desire*, you will see how you can introduce a faint impulse of intention in this field, and the creation of your desires will come about spontaneously. But first, you have to experience stillness. Stillness is the first requirement for manifesting your desires, because in stillness lies your connection to the field of pure potentiality that can orchestrate an infinity of details for you.

Imagine throwing a little stone into a still pond and watching it ripple. Then, after a while, when the ripples settle down, perhaps you throw another little stone. That's exactly what you do when you go into the field of pure silence and introduce your intention. In this silence, even the faintest intention will ripple across the underlying ground of universal consciousness, which connects everything with everything else. But, if you do not experience stillness in consciousness, if your mind is like a turbulent ocean, you could throw the Empire State Building into it, and you wouldn't notice a thing. In the Bible is the expression, "Be still, and know that I am God." This can only be accomplished through meditation.

Another way to access the field of pure potentiality is through the practice of non-judgment. Judgment is the constant evaluation of things as right or wrong, good or bad. When you are constantly evaluating, classifying, labeling, analyzing, you create a lot of turbulence in your internal dialogue. This turbulence constricts the flow of energy between you and the field of pure potentiality. You literally squeeze the "gap" between thoughts.

The gap is your connection to the field of pure potentiality. It is that state of pure awareness, that silent space between thoughts, that inner stillness that connects you to true power. And when you squeeze the gap, you squeeze your connection to the field of pure potentiality and infinite creativity.

There is a prayer in *A Course in Miracles* that states, "Today I shall judge nothing that occurs." Non-judgment creates silence in your mind. It is a good idea, therefore, to begin your day with that statement. And throughout the day, remind yourself of that statement each time you catch yourself judging. If practicing this procedure for the whole day seems too difficult, then you may simply say to yourself, "For the next two hours, I won't judge anything," or "For the next hour, I will experience non-judgment." Then you can extend it gradually.

Through silence, through meditation, and through non-judgment, you will access the first law, the *Law of Pure Potentiality*. Once you start doing that, you can add a fourth component to this practice, and that is regularly spending time in direct communion with nature. Spending time in nature enables you to sense the harmonious interaction of all the elements and forces of life, and gives you a sense of unity with all of life. Whether it be a stream, a forest, a mountain, a lake, or the seashore, that connection with nature's intelligence will also help you access the field of pure potentiality.

You must learn to get in touch with the innermost essence of your being. This true essence is beyond the ego. It is fearless; it is free; it is immune to criticism; it does not fear any challenge. It is beneath no one, superior to no one, and full of magic, mystery, and enchantment.

Access to your true essence will also give you insight into the mirror of relationship, because all relationship is a reflection of your relationship with yourself. For example, if you have guilt, fear, and insecurity over money, or success, or anything else, then these are reflections of guilt, fear, and insecurity as basic aspects of your personality. No amount of money or success will solve these basic problems of existence; only intimacy with the Self will bring about true healing. And when you are grounded in the knowledge of your true Self — when you really understand your true nature — you will never feel guilty, fearful, or insecure about money, or affluence, or fulfilling your desires, because you will realize that the essence of all material wealth is life energy, it is pure potentiality. And pure potentiality is your intrinsic nature.

As you gain more and more access to your true nature, you will also spontaneously receive creative thoughts, because the field of pure potentiality is also the field of infinite creativity and pure knowledge. Franz Kafka, the Austrian philosopher and poet, once said, "You need not leave your room. Remain sitting at your table and listen. You need not even listen, simply wait. You need not even wait, just learn to become quiet, and still, and solitary. The world will freely offer itself to you to be unmasked. It has no choice; it will roll in ecstasy at your feet."

The affluence of the universe — the lavish display and abundance of the universe — is an expression of the creative mind of nature. The more tuned in you are to the mind of nature, the more you have access to its infinite, unbounded creativity. But first, you have to go beyond the turbulence of your internal dialogue to connect with that abundant, affluent, infinite, creative mind. And then you create the possibility of dynamic activity while at the same time carrying the stillness of the eternal, unbounded, creative mind. This exquisite combination of silent, unbounded, infinite mind along with dynamic, bounded, individual mind is the perfect balance of stillness and movement simultaneously that can create whatever you want. This coexistence of opposites — stillness and dynamism at the same time — makes you independent of situations, circumstances, people, and things.

When you quietly acknowledge this exquisite coexistence of opposites, you align yourself with the world of energy — the quantum soup, the non-material non-stuff that is the source of the material world. This world of energy is fluid, dynamic, resilient, changing, forever in motion. And yet it is also non-changing, still, quiet, eternal, and silent.

Stillness alone is the potentiality for creativity; movement alone is creativity restricted to a certain aspect of its expression. But the combination of movement and stillness enables you to unleash your creativity in *all* directions — wherever the power of your attention takes you.

Wherever you go in the midst of movement and activity, carry your stillness within you. Then the chaotic movement around you will never over-shadow your access to the reservoir of creativity, the field of pure potentiality.

APPLYING THE
LAW OF PURE POTENTIALITY

I will put the *Law of Pure Potentiality* into effect by making a commitment to take the following steps:

(1) I will get in touch with the field of pure potentiality by taking time each day to be silent, to just *Be*. I will also sit alone in silent meditation at least twice a day for approximately thirty minutes in the morning and thirty minutes in the evening.

(2) I will take time each day to commune with nature and to silently witness the intelligence within every living thing. I will sit silently and watch a sunset, or listen to the sound of the ocean or a stream, or simply smell the scent of a flower. In the ecstasy of my own silence, and by

communing with nature, I will enjoy the life throb of ages, the field of pure potentiality and unbounded creativity.

(3) I will practice non-judgment. I will begin my day with the statement, "Today, I shall judge nothing that occurs," and throughout the day I will remind myself not to judge.

~ 2 ~

THE LAW OF GIVING

*The universe operates through dynamic
exchange . . . giving and receiving are different
aspects of the flow of energy in the universe.*

*And in our willingness to give that
which we seek, we keep the abundance of
the universe circulating in our lives.*

This frail vessel thou emptiest again and again, and fillest it ever with fresh life. This little flute of a reed thou hast carried over hills and dales, and hast breathed through it melodies eternally new. . . . Thy infinite gifts come to me only on those very small hands of mine. Ages pass, and still thou pourest, and still there is room to fill.

— *Rabindranath Tagore, Gitanjali*

The second spiritual law of success is the *Law of Giving*. This law could also be called the *Law of Giving and Receiving*, because the universe operates through dynamic exchange. Nothing is static. Your body is in dynamic and constant exchange with the body of the universe; your mind is dynamically interacting with the mind of the cosmos; your energy is an expression of cosmic energy.

The flow of life is nothing other than the harmonious interaction of all the elements and forces that structure the field of existence. This harmonious interaction of elements and forces in your life operates as the *Law of Giving*. Because your body and your mind and the universe are in constant and dynamic exchange, stopping the circulation of energy is like stopping the flow of blood. Whenever blood stops flowing, it begins to clot, to coagulate, to stagnate. That is why you must give and receive in order to keep wealth and affluence — or anything you want in life — circulating in your life.

The word affluence comes from the root word "affluere," which means "to flow to." The word affluence means "to flow in abundance." Money is really a symbol of the life energy we exchange and the life energy we use as a result of the service we provide to the universe. Another word for money is "currency," which also reflects the flowing nature of energy. The word currency comes from the Latin word "currere" which means "to run" or to flow.

Therefore, if we stop the circulation of money — if our only intention is to hold on to our money and hoard it — since it is life energy, we will stop its circulation back into our lives as well. In order to keep that energy coming to us, we have to keep the energy circulating. Like a river, money must keep flowing, otherwise it begins to stagnate, to clog, to suffocate and strangle its very own life force. Circulation keeps it alive and vital.

Every relationship is one of give and take. Giving engenders receiving, and receiving engenders giving. What goes up must come down; what goes out must come back. In reality, receiving is the same thing as giving, because giving and receiving are different aspects of the flow of energy in the universe. And if you stop the flow of either, you interfere with nature's intelligence.

In every seed is the promise of thousands of forests. But the seed must not be hoarded; it must give its intelligence to the fertile ground. Through its giving, its unseen energy flows into material manifestation.

The more you give, the more you will receive, because you will keep the abundance of the universe circulating in your life. In fact, anything that is of value in life only multiplies when it is given. That which doesn't multiply through giving is neither worth giving nor worth receiving. If, through the act of giving, you feel you have lost something, then the gift is not truly given and will not cause increase. If you give grudgingly, there is no energy behind that giving.

It is the intention behind your giving and receiving that is the most important thing. The intention should always be to create happiness for the giver and receiver, because happiness is life-supporting and life-sustaining and therefore generates increase. The return is directly proportional to the giving when it is unconditional and from the heart. That is why the act of giving has to be joyful — the frame of mind has to be one in which you feel joy in the *very act* of giving. Then the energy behind the giving increases many times over.

Practicing the *Law of Giving* is actually very simple: if you want joy, give joy to others; if you want love, learn to give love; if you want attention and appreciation, learn to give attention and appreciation; if you want material affluence, help others to become materially affluent. In fact, the easiest way to get what you want is to help others get what they want. This principle works equally well for individuals, corporations, societies, and nations. If you want to be blessed with all the good things in life, learn to silently bless everyone with all the good things in life.

Even the thought of giving, the thought of blessing, or a *simple prayer* has the power to affect others. This is because our body, reduced to its essential state, is a localized bundle of energy and information in a universe of energy and information. We are localized bundles of consciousness in a conscious universe. The word "consciousness" implies more than just energy and information — it implies energy and information which is alive as thought. Therefore we are bundles of thought in a thinking universe. And thought has the power to transform.

Life is the eternal dance of consciousness that expresses itself as the dynamic exchange of impulses of intelligence between microcosm and macrocosm, between the human body and the universal body, between the human mind and the cosmic mind.

When you learn to give that which you seek, you activate and choreograph the dance with an exquisite, energetic, and vital movement that constitutes the eternal throb of life.

The best way to put the *Law of Giving* into operation — to start the whole process of circulation — is to make a decision that any time you come into contact with anyone, you will give them something. It doesn't have to be in the form of material things; it could be a flower, a compliment, or a prayer. In fact, the most powerful forms of giving are nonmaterial. The gifts of caring, attention, affection, appreciation, and love are some of the most precious gifts you can give, and they don't cost you anything.

When you meet someone, you can silently send them a blessing, wishing them happiness, joy, and laughter. This kind of silent giving is very powerful.

One of the things I was taught as a child, and which I taught my children also, is never to go to anyone's house without bringing something — never visit anyone without bringing them a gift. You may say, "How can I give to others when at the moment I don't have enough myself?" You can bring a flower. One flower. You can bring a note or a card which says something about your feelings for the person you're visiting. You can bring a compliment. You can bring a prayer.

Make a decision to give wherever you go, to whomever you see. As long as you're giving, you will be receiving. The more you give, the more confidence you will gain in the miraculous effects of this law. And as you receive more, your ability to give more will also increase.

Our true nature is one of affluence and abundance; we are naturally affluent because nature supports every need and desire. We lack nothing, because our essential nature is one of pure potentiality and infinite possibilities. Therefore, you must know that you are already inherently affluent, no matter how much or how little money you have, because the source of all wealth is the field of pure potentiality — it is the consciousness that knows how to fulfill every need, including joy, love, laughter, peace, harmony, and knowledge. If you seek these things first — not only for yourself, but for others — all else will come to you spontaneously.

APPLYING THE
LAW OF GIVING

I will put the *Law of Giving* into effect by making a commitment to take the following steps:

(1) Wherever I go, and whoever I encounter, I will bring them a gift. The gift may be a compliment, a flower, or a prayer. Today, I will give something to everyone I come into contact with, and so I will begin the process of circulating joy, wealth and affluence in my life and in the lives of others.

(2) Today I will gratefully receive all the gifts that life has to offer me. I will receive the gifts of nature: sunlight and the sound of birds singing, or spring showers or the first snow of winter. I will also be open to receiving from others,

whether it be in the form of a material gift, money, a compliment, or a prayer.

(3) I will make a commitment to keep wealth circulating in my life by giving and receiving life's most precious gifts: the gifts of caring, affection, appreciation, and love. Each time I meet someone, I will silently wish them happiness, joy, and laughter.

~ 3 ~

THE LAW OF "KARMA" OR CAUSE AND EFFECT

Every action generates a force of energy
that returns to us in like kind . . .
what we sow is what we reap.

And when we choose actions that bring
happiness and success to others,
the fruit of our karma is happiness and success.

Karma is the eternal assertion of human free-dom. . . . Our thoughts, our words, and deeds are the threads of the net which we throw around ourselves.

— Swami Vivekananda

The third spiritual law of success is the *Law of Karma*. "Karma" is both action and the consequence of that action; it is cause and effect simultaneously, because every action generates a force of energy that returns to us in like kind. There is nothing unfamiliar about the *Law of Karma*. Everyone has heard the expression, "What you sow is what you reap." Obviously, if we want to create happiness in our lives, we must learn to sow the seeds of happiness. Therefore, karma implies the action of conscious choice-making.

You and I are essentially infinite choice-makers. In every moment of our existence, we are in that field of all possibilities where we have access to an infinity of choices. Some of these choices are made consciously, while others are made unconsciously. But the best way to understand and maximize the use of karmic law is to become consciously aware of the choices we make in every moment.

Whether you like it or not, everything that is happening at this moment is a result of the choices you've made in the past. Unfortunately, a lot of us make choices unconsciously, and therefore we don't think they are choices — and yet, they are.

If I were to insult you, you would most likely make the choice of being offended. If I were to pay you a compliment, you would most likely make the choice of being pleased or flattered. But think about it: it's still a choice.

I could offend you and I could insult you, and you could make the choice of not being offended. I could pay you a compliment and you could make the choice of not letting that flatter you either.

In other words, most of us — even though we are infinite choice-makers — have become bundles of conditioned reflexes that are constantly being triggered by people and circumstances into predictable outcomes of behavior. These conditioned reflexes are like Pavlovian conditioning. Pavlov is famous for demonstrating that if you give a dog something to eat every time you ring a bell, soon the dog starts to salivate when you just ring the bell, because it has associated one stimulus with the other.

Most of us, as a result of conditioning, have repetitious and predictable responses to the stimuli in our environment. Our reactions seem to be automatically triggered by people and circumstances, and we forget that these are still choices that we are making in every moment of our existence. We are simply making these choices unconsciously.

If you step back for a moment and witness the choices you are making as you make those choices, then in just this act of witnessing, you take the whole process from the unconscious realm into the conscious realm. This procedure of conscious choice-making and witnessing is very empowering.

When you make any choice — any choice at all — you can ask yourself two things: First of all, "What are the consequences of this choice that I'm making?" In your heart you will immediately know what these are. Secondly, "Will this choice that I'm making now bring happiness to me and to those around me?" If the answer is yes, then go ahead with that choice. If the answer is no, if that choice brings distress either to you or to those around you, then don't make that choice. It's as simple as that.

There is only one choice, out of the infinity of choices available in every second, that will create happiness for you as well as for those around you. And when you make that one choice, it will result in a form of behavior that is called spontaneous right action. Spontaneous right action is the right action at the right moment. It's the right response to every situation as it happens. It's the action that nourishes you and everyone else who is influenced by that action.

There is a very interesting mechanism that the universe has to help you make spontaneously correct choices. The mechanism has to do with sensations in your body. Your body experiences two kinds of sensations: one is a sensation of comfort, the other is a sensation of discomfort. At the moment you consciously make a choice, pay attention to your body and ask your body, "If I make this choice, what happens?" If your body sends a message of comfort, that's the right choice. If your body sends a message of discomfort, then it's not the appropriate choice.

For some people the message of comfort and discomfort is in the area of the solar plexus, but for most people it's in the area of the heart. Consciously put your attention in the heart and ask your heart what to do. Then wait for the response — a physical response in the form of a sensation. It may be the *faintest* level of feeling — but it's there, in your body.

Only the heart knows the correct answer. Most

people think the heart is mushy and sentimental. But it's not. The heart is intuitive; it's holistic, it's contextual, it's relational. It doesn't have a win-lose orientation. It taps into the cosmic computer — the field of pure potentiality, pure knowledge, and infinite organizing power — and takes everything into account. At times it may not even seem rational, but the heart has a computing ability that is far more accurate and far more precise than anything within the limits of rational thought.

You can use the *Law of Karma* to create money and affluence, and the flow of all good things to you, any time you want. But first, you must become consciously aware that your future is generated by the choices you are making in every moment of your life. If you do this on a regular basis, then you are making full use of the *Law of Karma*. The more you bring your choices into the level of your conscious awareness, the more you will make those choices which are spontaneously correct — both for you and those around you.

⌒ ⌒ ⌒

What about past karma and how it is influencing you now? There are three things you can do about past karma. One is to pay your karmic debts. Most people choose to do that — unconsciously, of course. This may be a choice you make, also. Sometimes there's a lot of suffering involved in the payment of those debts, but the *Law of Karma* says no debt in the universe ever goes unpaid. There is a perfect accounting system in this universe, and everything is a constant "to and fro" exchange of energy.

The second thing you can do is to transmute or transform your karma to a more desirable experience. This is a very interesting process in which you ask yourself, as you're paying your karmic debt, "What can I learn from this experience? Why is this happening and what is the message that the universe is giving to me? How can I make this experience useful to my fellow human beings?"

By doing this, you look for the seed of opportunity and then tie that seed of opportunity with your *dharma,* with your purpose in life, which we'll talk about in the Seventh Spiritual Law of Success. This allows you to transmute the karma to a new expression.

For example, if you break your leg while playing sports, you might ask, "What can I learn from this experience? What is the message that the universe is giving me?" Perhaps the message is that you need to slow down and be more careful or attentive to your body the next time. And if your dharma is to teach others what you know, then by asking, "How can I make this experience useful to my fellow human beings?" you may decide to share what you learned by writing a book about playing sports safely. Or you may design a special shoe or leg support that prevents the kind of injury you experienced.

This way, while paying your karmic debt, you will have also converted the adversity into a benefit that may bring you wealth and fulfillment. This is the transmutation of your karma into a positive experience. You haven't really gotten rid of your karma, but you are able to take a karmic episode and create a new and positive karma out of it.

The third way to deal with karma is to transcend it. To transcend karma is to become independent of it. The way to transcend karma is to keep experiencing the gap, the Self, the Spirit. It's like washing a dirty piece of cloth in a stream of water. Every time you wash it, you take away a few stains. You keep washing it again and again, and each time it gets a little cleaner. You wash or transcend the seeds of your karma by going into the gap and coming out again. This, of course, is done through the practice of meditation.

All actions are karmic episodes. Drinking a cup of coffee is a karmic episode. That action generates memory, and memory has the ability or the potentiality to generate desire. And desire generates action again. The operational software of your soul is karma, memory, and desire. Your soul is a bundle of consciousness that has the seeds of karma, memory, and desire. By becoming conscious of these seeds of manifestation, you become a conscious generator of reality. By becoming a conscious choice-maker, you begin to generate actions that are evolutionary for you and for those that are around you. And that's all you need to do.

As long as karma is evolutionary — for both the Self and everyone affected by the Self — then the fruit of karma will be happiness and success.

Applying The Law of "Karma" or Cause and Effect

I will put the *Law of Karma* into effect by making a commitment to take the following steps:

(1) Today I will witness the choices I make in each moment. And in the mere witnessing of these choices, I will bring them to my conscious awareness. I will know that the best way to prepare for any moment in the future is to be fully conscious in the present.

(2) Whenever I make a choice, I will ask myself two questions: "What are the consequences of this choice that I'm making?" and "Will this choice bring fulfillment and happiness to me and also to those who are affected by this choice?"

(3) I will then ask my heart for guidance and be guided by its message of comfort or discomfort. If the choice feels comfortable, I will plunge ahead with abandon. If the choice feels uncomfortable, I will pause and see the consequences of my action with my inner vision. This guidance will enable me to make spontaneously correct choices for myself and for all those around me.

~ 4 ~

THE LAW
OF LEAST EFFORT

Nature's intelligence functions with effortless ease . . . with carefreeness, harmony, and love.

And when we harness the forces of harmony, joy, and love, we create success and good fortune with effortless ease.

An integral being knows without going, sees without looking, and accomplishes without doing.

— Lao Tzu

The fourth spiritual law of success is the *Law of Least Effort*. This law is based on the fact that nature's intelligence functions with effortless ease and abandoned carefreeness. This is the principle of least action, of no resistance. This is, therefore, the principle of harmony and love. When we learn this lesson from nature, we easily fulfill our desires.

If you observe nature at work, you will see that least effort is expended. Grass doesn't try to grow, it just grows. Fish don't try to swim, they just swim. Flowers don't try to bloom, they bloom. Birds don't try to fly, they fly. This is their intrinsic nature. The earth doesn't try to spin on its own axis; it is the nature of the earth to spin with dizzying speed and to hurtle through space. It is the nature of babies to be in bliss. It is the nature of the sun to shine. It is the nature of the stars to glitter and sparkle. And it is human nature to make our dreams manifest into physical form, easily and effortlessly.

In Vedic Science, the age-old philosophy of India, this principle is known as the principle of economy of effort, or "do less and accomplish more." Ultimately you come to the state where you do nothing and accomplish everything. This means that there is just a faint idea, and then the manifestation of the idea comes about effortlessly. What is commonly called a "miracle" is actually an expression of the *Law of Least Effort.*

Nature's intelligence functions effortlessly, frictionlessly, spontaneously. It is non-linear; it is intuitive, holistic, and nourishing. And when you are in harmony with nature, when you are established in the knowledge of your true Self, you can make use of the *Law of Least Effort*.

Least effort is expended when your actions are motivated by love, because nature is held together by the energy of love. When you seek power and control over other people, you waste energy. When you seek money or power for the sake of the ego, you spend energy chasing the illusion of happiness instead of enjoying happiness in the moment. When you seek money for personal gain only, you cut off the flow of energy to yourself, and interfere with the expression of nature's intelligence. But when your actions are motivated by love, there is no waste of energy. When your actions are motivated by love, your energy multiplies and accumulates — and the surplus energy you gather and enjoy can be channeled to create anything that you want, including unlimited wealth.

You can think of your physical body as a device for controlling energy: it can generate, store, and expend energy. If you know how to generate, store, and expend energy in an efficient way, then you can create any amount of wealth. Attention to the ego consumes the greatest amount of energy. When your internal reference point is the ego, when you seek power and control over other people or seek approval from others, you spend energy in a wasteful way.

When that energy is freed up, it can be rechanneled and used to create anything that you want. When your internal reference point is your spirit, when you are immune to criticism and unfearful of any challenge, you can harness the power of love, and use energy creatively for the experience of affluence and evolution.

In *The Art of Dreaming*, Don Juan tells Carlos Castaneda, ". . . most of our energy goes into upholding our importance. . . . If we were capable of losing some of that importance, two extraordinary things would happen to us. One, we would free our energy from trying to maintain the illusory idea of our grandeur; and two, we would provide ourselves with enough energy to . . . catch a glimpse of the actual grandeur of the universe."

There are three components to the *Law of Least Effort* — three things you can do to put this principle of "do less and accomplish more" into action. The first component is acceptance. Acceptance simply means that you make a commitment: "Today I will accept people, situations, circumstances, and events as they occur." This means I will know that *this moment is as it should be*, because the whole universe is as it should be. This moment — the one you're experiencing right now — is the culmination of all the moments you have experienced in the past. This moment is as it is because the entire universe is as it is.

When you struggle against this moment, you're actually struggling against the entire universe. Instead, you can make the decision that today you will not struggle against the whole universe by struggling against this moment. This means that your *acceptance* of this moment is total and complete. You accept things as they *are*, not as you wish they were in this moment. This is important to understand. You can *wish* for things in the future to be different, but in *this* moment you have to accept things as they are.

When you feel frustrated or upset by a person or a situation, remember that you are not reacting to the person or the situation, but to your feelings about the person or the situation. These are *your* feelings, and your feelings are not someone else's fault. When you recognize and understand this completely, you are ready to take responsibility for how you feel and to change it. And if you can accept things as they are, you are ready to take responsibility for your situation and for all the events you see as problems.

This leads us to the second component of the *Law of Least Effort*: responsibility. What does responsibility mean? Responsibility means not blaming anyone or anything for your situation, including yourself. Having accepted this circumstance, this event, this problem, responsibility then means the *ability* to have a creative *response* to the situation *as it is now.* All problems contain the seeds of opportunity, and this awareness allows you to take the moment and transform it to a better situation or thing.

Once you do this, every so-called upsetting situation will become an opportunity for the creation of something new and beautiful, and every so-called tormentor or tyrant will become your teacher. Reality is an interpretation. And if you choose to interpret reality in this way, you will have many teachers around you, and many opportunities to evolve.

Whenever confronted by a tyrant, tormentor, teacher, friend, or foe (they all mean the same thing) remind yourself, "This moment is as it should be." Whatever relationships you have attracted in your life at this moment are precisely the ones you need in your life at this moment. There is a hidden meaning behind all events, and this hidden meaning is serving your own evolution.

The third component of the *Law of Least Effort* is defenselessness, which means that your awareness is established in defenselessness, and you have relinquished the need to convince or persuade others of your point of view. If you observe people around you, you'll see that they spend ninety-nine percent of their time defending their points of view. If you just relinquish the need to defend your point of view, you will in that relinquishment, gain access to enormous amounts of energy that have been previously wasted.

When you become defensive, blame others, and do not accept and surrender to the moment, your life meets resistance. Any time you encounter resistance, recognize that if you force the situation, the resistance will only increase. You don't want to stand rigid like a tall oak that cracks and collapses in the storm. Instead, you want to be flexible, like a reed that bends with the storm and survives.

Completely desist from defending your point of view. When you have no point to defend, you do not allow the birth of an argument. If you do this consistently — if you stop fighting and resisting — you will fully experience the present, which is a gift. Someone once told me, "The past is history, the future is a mystery, and this moment is a gift. That is why this moment is called 'the present'."

If you embrace the present and become one with it, and merge with it, you will experience a fire, a glow, a sparkle of ecstasy throbbing in every living sentient being. As you begin to experience this exultation of spirit in everything that is alive, as you become intimate with it, joy will be born within you, and you will drop the terrible burdens and encumbrances of defensiveness, resentment, and hurtfulness. Only then will you become lighthearted, carefree, joyous, and free.

In this joyful, simple freedom, you will know without any doubt in your heart that what you want is available to you whenever you want it, because your want will be from the level of happiness, not from the level of anxiety or fear. You do not need to justify; simply declare your intent to yourself, and you will experience fulfillment, delight, joy, freedom, and autonomy in every moment of your life.

Make a commitment to follow the path of no resistance. This is the path through which nature's intelligence unfolds spontaneously, without friction or effort. When you have the exquisite combination of acceptance, responsibility, and defenselessness, you will experience life flowing with effortless ease.

When you remain open to all points of view — not rigidly attached to only one — your dreams and desires will flow with nature's desires. Then you can release your intentions, without attachment, and just wait for the appropriate season for your desires to blossom into reality. You can be sure that when the season is right, your desires will manifest. This is the *Law of Least Effort*.

Applying The
Law of Least Effort

I will put the *Law of Least Effort* into effect by making a commitment to take the following steps:

(1) I will practice *Acceptance*. Today I will accept people, situations, circumstances, and events as they occur. I will know that *this moment is as it should be*, because the whole universe is as it should be. I will not struggle against the whole universe by struggling against this moment. My acceptance is total and complete. I accept things as they are this moment, not as I wish they were.

(2) Having accepted things as they are, I will take *Responsibility* for my situation and for all those events I see as problems. I know that taking responsibility means not blaming anyone or

anything for my situation (and this includes myself). I also know that every problem is an opportunity in disguise, and this alertness to opportunities allows me to take this moment and transform it into a greater benefit.

(3) Today my awareness will remain established in *Defenselessness*. I will relinquish the need to defend my point of view. I will feel no need to convince or persuade others to accept my point of view. I will remain open to all points of view and not be rigidly attached to any one of them.

☙ 5 ☙

THE LAW OF
INTENTION AND DESIRE

*Inherent in every intention and desire is the
mechanics for its fulfillment . . . intention
and desire in the field of pure potentiality
have infinite organizing power.*

*And when we introduce an intention in
the fertile ground of pure potentiality, we put
this infinite organizing power to work for us.*

In the beginning there was desire, which was the first seed of mind; sages, having meditated in their hearts, have discovered by their wisdom the connection of the existent with the non-existent.

— *The Hymn of Creation, The Rig Veda*

The fifth spiritual law of success is the *Law of Intention and Desire*. This law is based on the fact that energy and information exist everywhere in nature. In fact, at the level of the quantum field, there is nothing other than energy and information. The quantum field is just another label for the field of pure consciousness or pure potentiality. And this quantum field is influenced by intention and desire. Let's examine this process in detail.

A flower, a rainbow, a tree, a blade of grass, a human body, when broken down to their essential components, are energy and information. The whole universe, in its essential nature, is the *movement* of energy and information. The only difference between you and a tree is the informational and energy content of your respective bodies.

On the material level, both you and the tree are made up of the same recycled elements: mostly carbon, hydrogen, oxygen, nitrogen, and other elements in minute amounts. You could buy these elements in a hardware store for a couple of dollars. The difference, therefore, between you and the tree is not the carbon, or the hydrogen, or the oxygen. In fact, you and the tree are constantly exchanging your carbon and oxygen with each other. The real difference between the two of you is in the energy and in the information.

In the scheme of nature, you and I are a privileged species. We have a nervous system that is capable of becoming *aware* of the energy and informational content of that localized field that gives rise to our physical body. We *experience* this field subjectively as our own thoughts, feelings, emotions, desires, memories, instincts, drives, and beliefs. This same field is experienced objectively as the physical body — and through the physical body, we experience this field as the world. But it's all the same stuff. That is why the ancient seers exclaimed, "I am that, you are that, all this is that, and that's all there is."

Your body is not separate from the body of the universe, because at quantum mechanical levels there are no well-defined edges. You are like a wiggle, a wave, a fluctuation, a convolution, a whirlpool, a localized disturbance in the larger quantum field. The larger quantum field — the universe — is your extended body.

Not only is the human nervous system capable of becoming aware of the information and energy of its own quantum field, but because human consciousness is infinitely flexible through this wonderful nervous system, you are able to consciously change the informational content that gives rise to your physical body. You can consciously change the energy and informational content of your *own* quantum mechanical body, and therefore influence the energy and informational content of your extended body — your environment, your world — and cause things to manifest in it.

This conscious change is brought about by the two qualities inherent in consciousness: attention and intention. Attention energizes, and intention transforms. Whatever you put your attention on will grow stronger in your life. Whatever you take your attention away from will wither, disintegrate, and disappear. Intention, on the other hand, triggers transformation of energy and information. Intention organizes its own fulfillment.

The quality of *intention* on the object of *attention* will orchestrate an infinity of space-time events to bring about the outcome intended, provided one follows the other spiritual laws of success. This is because intention in the fertile ground of attention has infinite organizing power. Infinite organizing power means the power to organize an infinity of space-time events, all at the same time. We see the expression of this infinite organizing power in every blade of grass, in every apple blossom, in every cell of our body. We see it in everything that is alive.

In the scheme of nature, everything correlates and connects with everything else. The groundhog comes out of the earth and you know it is going to be spring. Birds begin to migrate in a certain direction at a certain time of the year. Nature is a symphony. And that symphony is being silently orchestrated at the ultimate ground of creation.

The human body is another good example of this symphony. A single cell in the human body is doing about six trillion things per second, and it has to know what every other cell is doing at the same time. The human body can play music, kill germs, make a baby, recite poetry, and monitor the movement of stars all at the same time, because the field of infinite correlation is part of its information field.

What is remarkable about the nervous system of the human species is that it can command this infinite organizing power through conscious intent. Intent in the human species is not fixed or locked into a rigid network of energy and information. It has infinite flexibility. In other words, as long as you do not violate the other laws of nature, through your intent you can literally command the laws of nature to fulfill your dreams and desires.

You can put the cosmic computer with its infinite organizing power to work for you. You can go to that ultimate ground of creation and introduce an intention, and just by introducing the intention, you activate the field of infinite correlation.

Intention lays the groundwork for the effortless, spontaneous, frictionless flow of pure potentiality seeking expression from the unmanifest to the manifest. The only caution is that you use your intent for the benefit of mankind. This happens spontaneously when you are in alignment with The Seven Spiritual Laws of Success.

⌒ ⌒ ⌒

Intention is the real power behind desire. Intent alone is very powerful, because intent is desire without attachment to the outcome. Desire alone is weak, because desire in most people is attention with attachment. Intent is desire with strict adherence to all the other laws, but particularly the *Law of Detachment*, which is the Sixth Spiritual Law of Success.

Intention combined with detachment leads to life-centered, present-moment awareness. And when action is performed in present-moment awareness, it is most effective. Your *intent* is for the future, but your *attention* is in the present. As long as your attention is in the present, then your intent for the future will manifest, because the future is created in the present. You must accept the present as is. Accept the present and intend the future. The future is something you can always create through detached intention, but you should never struggle against the present.

The past, present, and future are all properties of consciousness. The past is recollection, memory;

the future is anticipation; the present is awareness. Therefore time is the movement of thought. Both past and future are born in the imagination; only the present, which is awareness, is real and eternal. It is. It is the potentiality for space-time, matter, and energy. It is an eternal field of possibilities experiencing itself as abstract forces, whether they be light, heat, electricity, magnetism, or gravity. These forces are neither in the past nor in the future. They just are.

Our interpretation of these abstract forces gives us the experience of concrete phenomena and form. Remembered interpretations of abstract forces create the experience of the past, anticipatory interpretations of the same abstract forces create the future. They are the qualities of attention in consciousness. When these qualities are freed from the burden of the past, then action in the present becomes the fertile ground for the creation of the future.

Intention, grounded in this detached freedom of the present, serves as the catalyst for the right mix of matter, energy, and space-time events to create whatever it is that you desire.

If you have life-centered, present-moment awareness, then the imaginary obstacles — which are more than ninety percent of perceived obstacles — disintegrate and disappear. The remaining five to ten percent of perceived obstacles can be transmuted into opportunities through one-pointed intention.

One-pointed intention is that quality of attention that is unbending in its fixity of purpose. One-pointed intention means holding your attention to the intended outcome with such unbending purpose that you absolutely refuse to allow obstacles to consume and dissipate the focused quality of your attention. There is a total and complete exclusion of all obstacles from your consciousness. You are able to maintain an unshakable serenity while being committed to your goal with intense passion. This is the power of detached awareness and one-pointed, focused intention simultaneously.

Learn to harness the power of intention, and you

can create anything you desire. You can still get results through effort and through trying, but at a cost. The cost is stress, heart attacks, and the compromised function of your immune system. It is much better to execute the following five steps in the *Law of Intention and Desire*. When you follow these five steps for fulfilling your desires, intention generates its own power:

(1) Slip into the gap. This means to center yourself in that silent space between thoughts, to go into the silence — that level of Being which is your essential state.

(2) Established in that state of Being, release your intentions and desires. When you are actually in the gap, there's no thought, there's no intention, but as you come out of the gap — at that junction between the gap and a thought — you introduce the intention. If you have a series of goals, you can write them down, and have your

intention focused on them before you go into the gap. If you want a successful career, for example, you go into the gap with that intention, and the intention will already be there as a faint flicker in your awareness. Releasing your intentions and desires in the gap means planting them in the fertile ground of pure potentiality, and expecting them to bloom when the season is right. You do not want to dig up the seeds of your desires to see if they are growing, or get rigidly attached to the way in which they will unfold. You simply want to release them.

(3) Remain in the state of self-referral. This means remain established in the awareness of your true Self — your spirit, your connection to the field of pure potentiality. It also means not to look at yourself through the eyes of the world, or allow yourself to be influenced by the opinions and criticisms of others. A helpful way to maintain that state of self-referral is to keep your desires

to yourself; do not share them with anyone else unless they share the exact same desires that you have and are closely bonded with you.

(4) Relinquish your attachment to the outcome. This means giving up your rigid attachment to a specific result and living in the wisdom of uncertainty. It means enjoying every moment in the journey of your life, even if you don't know the outcome.

(5) Let the universe handle the details. Your intentions and desires, when released in the gap, have infinite organizing power. Trust that infinite organizing power of intention to orchestrate all the details for you.

Remember that your true nature is one of pure spirit. Carry the consciousness of your spirit wherever you go, gently release your desires, and the universe will handle the details for you.

APPLYING THE
LAW OF INTENTION AND DESIRE

I will put the *Law of Intention and Desire* into effect by making a commitment to take the following steps:

(1) I will make a list of all my desires. I will carry this list with me wherever I go. I will look at this list before I go into my silence and meditation. I will look at it before I go to sleep at night. I will look at it when I wake up in the morning.

(2) I will release this list of my desires and surrender it to the womb of creation, trusting that when things don't seem to go my way, there is a reason, and that the cosmic plan has designs for me much grander than even those that I have conceived.

(3) I will remind myself to practice present-moment awareness in all my actions. I will refuse to allow obstacles to consume and dissipate the quality of my attention in the present moment. I will accept the present *as it is*, and manifest the future through my deepest, most cherished intentions and desires.

ᴄ 6 ᕽ

THE LAW
OF DETACHMENT

*In detachment lies the wisdom of uncertainty . . .
in the wisdom of uncertainty lies the freedom
from our past, from the known,
which is the prison of past conditioning.*

*And in our willingness to step into the
unknown, the field of all possibilities,
we surrender ourselves to the creative mind
that orchestrates the dance of the universe.*

Like two golden birds perched on the selfsame tree, intimate friends, the ego and the Self dwell in the same body. The former eats the sweet and sour fruits of the tree of life, while the latter looks on in detachment.

— The Mundaka Upanishad

The sixth spiritual law of success is the *Law of Detachment*. The *Law of Detachment* says that in order to acquire anything in the physical universe, you have to relinquish your attachment to it. This doesn't mean you give up the intention to create your desire. You don't give up the intention, and you don't give up the desire. You give up your attachment to the result.

This a very powerful thing to do. The moment you relinquish your attachment to the result, combining one-pointed intention with detachment at the same time, you will have that which you desire. Anything you want can be acquired through detachment, because detachment is based on the unquestioning belief in the power of your true Self.

Attachment, on the other hand, is based on fear and insecurity — and the need for security is based on not knowing the true Self. The source of wealth, of abundance, or of anything in the physical world is the Self; it is the consciousness that knows how to fulfill every need. Everything else is a symbol: cars, houses, bank notes, clothes, airplanes. Symbols are transitory; they come and go. Chasing symbols is like settling for the map instead of the territory. It creates anxiety; it ends up making you feel hollow and empty inside, because you exchange your Self for the *symbols* of your Self.

Attachment comes from poverty consciousness, because attachment is always to symbols. Detachment is synonymous with wealth consciousness, because with detachment there is freedom to create. Only from detached involvement can one have joy and laughter. Then the symbols of wealth are created spontaneously and effortlessly. Without detachment we are prisoners of helplessness, hopelessness, mundane needs, trivial concerns, quiet desperation, and seriousness — the distinctive features of everyday mediocre existence and poverty consciousness.

True wealth consciousness is the ability to have anything you want, anytime you want, and with least effort. To be grounded in this experience you have to be grounded in the wisdom of uncertainty. In this uncertainty you will find the freedom to create anything you want.

People are constantly seeking security, and you will find that seeking security is actually a very ephemeral thing. Even attachment to money is a sign of insecurity. You might say, "When I have X million dollars, then I'll be secure. Then I'll be financially independent and I will retire. Then I will do all the things I really want to do." But it never happens — *never* happens.

Those who seek security chase it for a lifetime

without ever finding it. It remains elusive and ephemeral, because security can never come from money alone. Attachment to money will always create insecurity no matter how much money you have in the bank. In fact, some of the people who have the most money are the most insecure.

The search for security is an illusion. In ancient wisdom traditions, the solution to this whole dilemma lies in the wisdom of insecurity, or the wisdom of uncertainty. This means that the search for security and certainty is actually an *attachment* to the known. And what's the known? The known is our past. The known is nothing other than the prison of past conditioning. There's no evolution in that — absolutely none at all. And when there is no evolution, there is stagnation, entropy, disorder, and decay.

Uncertainty, on the other hand, is the fertile ground of pure creativity and freedom. Uncertainty means stepping into the unknown in every moment of our existence. The unknown is the field of all possibilities, ever fresh, ever new, always open to the creation of new manifestations. Without uncertainty and the unknown, life is just the stale repetition of outworn memories. You become the victim of the past, and your tormentor today is your self left over from yesterday.

Relinquish your attachment to the known, step into the unknown, and you will step into the field of all possibilities. In your willingness to step into the unknown, you will have the wisdom of uncertainty factored in. This means that in every moment of your life, you will have excitement, adventure, mystery. You will experience the fun of life — the magic, the celebration, the exhilaration, and the exultation of your own spirit.

Every day you can look for the excitement of what may occur in the field of all possibilities. When you experience uncertainty, you are on the right path — so don't give it up. You don't need to have a complete and rigid idea of what you'll be doing next week or next year, because if you have a very clear idea of what's going to happen and you get rigidly attached to it, then you shut out a *whole range of possibilities*.

One characteristic of the field of all possibilities is infinite correlation. The field can orchestrate an infinity of space-time events to bring about the outcome that is intended. But when you are attached, your intention gets locked into a rigid mindset and you lose the fluidity, the creativity, and the spontaneity inherent in the field. When you get attached, you freeze your desire from that infinite fluidity and flexibility into a rigid framework which interferes with the whole process of creation.

The *Law of Detachment* does not interfere with the *Law of Intention and Desire* — with goal-setting. You still have the intention of going in a certain direction, you still have a goal. However, between point A and point B there are infinite possibilities. With uncertainty factored in, you might change direction in any moment if you find a higher ideal, or if you find something more exciting. You are also less likely to force solutions on problems, which enables you to stay alert to opportunities.

The *Law of Detachment* accelerates the whole process of evolution. When you understand this law, you don't feel compelled to force solutions. When you force solutions on problems, you only create new problems. But when you put your attention on the uncertainty, and you witness the uncertainty while you expectantly wait for the solution to emerge out of the chaos and the confusion, then what emerges is something very fabulous and exciting.

This state of alertness — your preparedness in the present, in the field of uncertainty — meets with your goal and your intention and allows you to seize the opportunity. What's the opportunity? It's contained within every problem that you have in your life. Every single problem that you have in your life is the seed of an opportunity for some greater benefit. Once you have that perception, you open up to a whole range of possibilities — and this keeps the mystery, the wonder, the excitement, the adventure alive.

You can look at every problem you have in your life as an opportunity for some greater benefit. You can stay alert to opportunities by being grounded in the wisdom of uncertainty. When your preparedness meets opportunity, the solution will spontaneously appear.

What comes out of that is often called "good luck." Good luck is nothing but preparedness and opportunity coming together. When the two are mixed together with an alert witnessing of the chaos, a solution emerges that will be of evolutionary bene-fit to you and to all those that you come into contact with. This is the perfect recipe for success, and it is based on the *Law of Detachment*.

APPLYING THE
LAW OF DETACHMENT

I will put the *Law of Detachment* into effect by making a commitment to take the following steps:

(1) Today I will commit myself to detachment. I will allow myself and those around me the freedom to be as they are. I will not rigidly impose my idea of how things should be. I will not force solutions on problems, thereby creating new problems. I will participate in everything with detached involvement.

(2) Today I will factor in uncertainty as an essential ingredient of my experience. In my willingness to accept uncertainty, solutions will spontaneously emerge out of the problem, out of the confusion, disorder, and chaos. The more

uncertain things seem to be, the more secure I will feel, because uncertainty is my path to freedom. Through the wisdom of uncertainty, I will find my security.

(3) I will step into the field of all possibilities and anticipate the excitement that can occur when I remain open to an infinity of choices. When I step into the field of all possibilities, I will experience all the fun, adventure, magic, and mystery of life.

~ 7 ~

THE LAW OF "DHARMA"
OR PURPOSE IN LIFE

*Everyone has a purpose in life . . . a unique
gift or special talent to give to others.*

*And when we blend this unique talent with
service to others, we experience the ecstasy
and exultation of our own spirit, which is
the ultimate goal of all goals.*

When you work you are a flute through whose heart the whispering of the hours turns to music. . . . And what is it to work with love? It is to weave the cloth with threads drawn from your heart, even as if your beloved were to wear that cloth. . . .

— Kahlil Gibran, The Prophet

The seventh spiritual law of success is the *Law of Dharma*. Dharma is a Sanskrit word that means "purpose in life." The *Law of Dharma* says that we have taken manifestation in physical form to fulfill a purpose. The field of pure potentiality is divinity in its essence, and the divine takes human form to fulfill a purpose.

According to this law, you have a unique talent and a unique way of expressing it. There is something that you can do better than anyone else in the whole world — and for every unique talent and unique expression of that talent, there are also unique needs. When these needs are matched with the creative expression of your talent, that is the spark that creates affluence. Expressing your talents to fulfill needs creates unlimited wealth and abundance.

If you could start children right from the beginning with this thought, you'd see the effect it has on their lives. In fact, I did this with my own children. Again and again, I told them there was a reason why they were here, and they had to find out what that reason was for themselves. From the age of four years, they *heard* this. I also taught them to meditate when they were about the same age, and I told them, "I never, ever want you to worry about making a living. If you're unable to make a living when you grow up, I'll provide for you, so don't worry about that. I don't want you to focus on doing well in school. I don't want you to focus on getting the best grades or going to the best colleges. What I really want you to focus on is asking yourself how you can serve humanity, and asking yourself what your unique talents are. Because you have a unique talent that no one else has, and you have a special way of expressing that talent, and no one else has it." They ended up going to the best schools, getting the best grades, and even in college, they are unique in that they are financially self-sufficient, because they are *focused on what they are here to give.* This then, is the *Law of Dharma.*

There are three components to the *Law of Dharma.* The first component says that each of us is here to discover our true Self, to find out on our own that our true Self is spiritual, that essentially we are spiritual beings that have taken manifestation in physical form. We're not human beings that have occasional spiritual experiences — it's the other way around: we're spiritual beings that have occasional human experiences.

Each of us is here to discover our higher self or our spiritual self. That's the first fulfillment of the

Law of Dharma. We must find out for ourself that inside us is a god or goddess in embryo that wants to be born so that we can express our divinity.

The second component of the *Law of Dharma* is to express our unique talents. The *Law of Dharma* says that every human being has a unique talent. You have a talent that is unique in its expression, so unique that there's no one else alive on this planet that has that talent, or that expression of that talent. This means that there's one thing you can do, and one way of doing it, that is better than anyone else on this entire planet. When you're doing that one thing, you lose track of time. When you're expressing that one unique talent that you possess — or more than one unique talent in many cases — the expression of that talent takes you into timeless awareness.

The third component of the *Law of Dharma* is service to humanity — to serve your fellow human beings and to ask yourself the questions, "How can I help? How can I help all those that I come into contact with?" When you combine the ability to express your unique talent with service to humanity, then you make full use of the *Law of Dharma*. And coupled with the experience of your own spirituality, the field of pure potentiality, there is *no way* you will not have access to unlimited abundance, because that is the *real* way abundance is achieved.

This is not a temporary abundance; it's permanent, because of your unique talent, your way of expressing it, and your service and dedication to your fellow human beings, which you discover through asking the question, "How can I help?" instead of "What's in it for me?"

The question, "What's in it for me?" is the internal dialogue of the ego. Asking "How can I help?" is the internal dialogue of the spirit. The spirit is that domain of your awareness where you experience your universality. In just shifting your internal dialogue from "What's in it for me?" to "How can I help?" you automatically go beyond the ego into the domain of your spirit. While meditation is the most useful way of entering the domain of spirit, simply shifting your internal dialogue to "How can I help?" will also access the spirit, that domain of your awareness where you experience your universality.

If you want to make maximum use of the *Law of Dharma*, then you have to make several commitments.

The first commitment is: I am going to seek my higher self, which is beyond my ego, through spiritual practice.

The second commitment is: I am going to discover my unique talents, and finding my unique talents, I am going to enjoy myself, because the process of enjoyment occurs when I go into timeless awareness. That's when I am in a state of bliss.

The third commitment is: I am going to ask myself how I am best suited to serve humanity. I am going to answer that question and then put it into practice. I am going to use my unique talents to serve the needs of my fellow human beings — I will match those needs to my desire to help and serve others.

Sit down and make a list of the answers to these two questions: Ask yourself, if money was no concern and you had all the time and money in the world, what would you do? If you would still do what you currently do, then you are in dharma, because you have *passion* for what you do — you are expressing your unique talents. Then ask yourself: How am I best suited to serve humanity? Answer that question, and put it into practice.

Discover your divinity, find your unique talent, serve humanity with it, and you can generate all the wealth that you want. When your creative expressions match the needs of your fellow humans, then wealth will spontaneously flow from the unmanifest into the manifest, from the realm of the spirit to the world of form. You will begin to experience your life as a miraculous expression of divinity — not just occasionally, but all the time. And you will know true joy and the true meaning of success — the ecstasy and exultation of your own spirit.

Applying The Law of "Dharma" or Purpose in Life

I will put the *Law of Dharma* into effect by making a commitment to take the following steps:

(1) Today I will lovingly nurture the god or goddess in embryo that lies deep within my soul. I will pay attention to the spirit within me that animates both my body and my mind. I will awaken myself to this deep stillness within my heart. I will carry the consciousness of timeless, eternal Being in the midst of time-bound experience.

(2) I will make a list of my unique talents. Then I will list all the things that I love to do while expressing my unique talents. When I express my unique talents and use them in the service of humanity, I lose track of time and create

abundance in my life as well as in the lives of others.

(3) I will ask myself daily, "How can I serve?" and "How can I help?" The answers to these questions will allow me to help and serve my fellow human beings with love.

SUMMARY AND CONCLUSION

I want to know God's thoughts . . . the rest are details.

— Albert Einstein

The universal mind choreographs everything that is happening in billions of galaxies with elegant precision and unfaltering intelligence. Its intelligence is ultimate and supreme, and it permeates every fiber of existence: from the smallest to the largest, from the atom to the cosmos. Everything that is alive is an expression of this intelligence. And this intelligence operates through The Seven Spiritual Laws.

If you look at any cell in the human body, you will see through its functioning the expression of these laws. Every cell, whether it's a stomach cell, or a heart cell, or a brain cell, has its birth in the *Law of Pure Potentiality*. DNA is a perfect example of pure potentiality; in fact, it is the *material expression* of pure potentiality. The same DNA existing in every cell expresses itself in different ways in order to fulfill the unique requirements of that particular cell.

Each cell also operates through the *Law of Giving*. A cell is alive and healthy when it is in a state of balance and equilibrium. This state of equilibrium is one of fulfillment and harmony, but it is maintained by a constant give and take. Each cell gives to and supports every other cell, and in turn is nourished by every other cell. The cell is always in a state of dynamic flow and the flow is never interrupted. In fact, the flow is the very essence of the life of the cell. And only by maintaining this flow of giving is the cell able to receive and thus continue its vibrant existence.

The *Law of Karma* is exquisitely executed by every cell, because built into its intelligence is the most appropriate and precisely correct response to every situation as it occurs.

The *Law of Least Effort* is also exquisitely executed by every cell in the body: it does its job with quiet efficiency in the state of restful alertness.

Through the *Law of Intention and Desire*, every intention of every cell harnesses the infinite organizing power of nature's intelligence. Even a simple intention such as metabolizing a molecule of sugar immediately sets off a symphony of events in the body where precise amounts of hormones have to be secreted at precise moments to convert this molecule of sugar into pure creative energy.

Of course, every cell expresses the *Law of Detachment*. It is detached from the outcome of its intentions. It doesn't stumble or falter because its behavior is a function of life-centered, present-moment awareness.

Each cell also expresses the *Law of Dharma*. Each cell must discover its own source, the higher self; it must serve its fellow beings, and express its unique talents. Heart cells, stomach cells, and immune cells all have their source in the higher self, the field of pure potentiality. And because they are directly linked to this cosmic computer, they can express their unique talents with effortless ease and timeless awareness. Only by expressing their unique talents can they maintain both their own integrity and the integrity of the whole body. The internal dialogue of every cell in the human body is, "How can I help?" The heart cells want to help the immune cells, the immune cells want to help the stomach and lung cells, and the brain cells are listening to and helping every other cell. Every cell in the human body has only one function: to help every other cell.

By looking at the behavior of the cells of our own body, we can observe the most extraordinary and efficient expression of The Seven Spiritual Laws. This is the genius of nature's intelligence. These are the thoughts of God — the rest are details.

☙ ☙ ☙

The Seven Spiritual Laws of Success are powerful principles that will enable you to attain self-mastery. If you put your attention on these laws and practice the steps outlined in this book, you will see that you can manifest anything you want — all the affluence, money, and success that you desire. You will also see that your life becomes more joyful and abundant in every way, for these laws are also the spiritual laws of life that make living worthwhile.

There is a natural sequence for the application of these laws in your daily life that may help you to remember them. The *Law of Pure Potentiality* is experienced through silence, through meditation, through non-judgment, through communion with nature, but it is activated by the *Law of Giving*. The principle here is to learn to give that which you seek. That's how you activate the *Law of Pure Potentiality*. If you seek affluence, give affluence; if you seek money, give money; if you seek love, appreciation, and affection, then learn to give love, appreciation, and affection.

Through your actions in the *Law of Giving* you activate the *Law of Karma*. You create good karma, and good karma makes everything in life easy. You notice that you don't have to expend a lot of effort to fulfill your desires, which automatically leads to an understanding of the *Law of Least Effort*. When everything is easy and effortless, and your desires keep getting fulfilled, you spontaneously begin to understand the *Law of Intention and Desire*. Fulfilling your desires with effortless ease makes it easy for you to practice the *Law of Detachment*.

Finally, as you begin to understand all the above laws, you begin to focus on your true purpose in life, which leads to the *Law of Dharma*. Through the use of this law, by expressing your unique talents and fulfilling the needs of your fellow humans, you begin to create whatever you want, whenever you want it. You become carefree and joyful, and your life becomes an expression of unbounded love.

We are travelers on a cosmic journey — stardust, swirling and dancing in the eddies and whirlpools of infinity. Life is eternal. But the expressions of life are ephemeral, momentary, transient. Gautama Buddha, the founder of Buddhism, once said,

> This existence of ours is as transient as autumn
>   clouds.
> To watch the birth and death of beings is like
>   looking at the movements of a dance.
> A lifetime is like a flash of lightning in the sky,
> Rushing by like a torrent down a steep mountain.

We have stopped for a moment to encounter each other, to meet, to love, to share. This is a precious moment, but it is transient. It is a little parenthesis in eternity. If we share with caring, lightheartedness, and love, we will create abundance and joy for each other. And then this moment will have been worthwhile.

ABOUT THE AUTHOR

Deepak Chopra is a world-renowned leader in the field of mind-body medicine and human potential. He is the bestselling author of numerous books, including *Ageless Body, Timeless Mind*; *Quantum Healing*; and *Creating Affluence*, as well as numerous audio and video programs that promote health and well-being. His books have been translated into more than twenty-five languages and he lectures widely throughout North America, South America, India, Europe, Japan, and Australia. Currently he is the Executive Director for the Institute of Mind-Body Medicine and Human Potential at Sharp HealthCare in San Diego, California.

ALSO FROM DEEPAK CHOPRA

BOOKS:

Creating Affluence (Amber-Allen / New World Library)

Ageless Body, Timeless Mind (Crown / Harmony)

Journey Into Healing (Crown / Harmony)

Restful Sleep (Crown / Harmony)

Perfect Weight (Crown / Harmony)

Perfect Health (Crown / Harmony)

Unconditional Life (Bantam)

Quantum Healing (Bantam)

Creating Health (Houghton Mifflin)

Return of the Rishi (Houghton Mifflin)

AUDIO CASSETTES:

The following audio cassettes are co-published by Amber-Allen Publishing and New World Library:

The Seven Spiritual Laws of Success

Creating Affluence

Escaping the Prison of the Intellect

Sacred Verses, Healing Sounds, Volume I
  The Bhagavad Gita

Sacred Verses, Healing Sounds, Volume II
  Hymns of the Rig Veda

Living Beyond Miracles (with Dr. Wayne Dyer)

Return of the Rishi

Other Audio Programs:

Magical Mind, Magical Body (Nightingale-Conant)
The Higher Self (Nightingale-Conant)
Unconditional Life (Bantam Audio Publishing)
Weight Loss: The Complete Mind-Body Solution
    (Quantum Publications, Inc.)
Insomnia: The Complete Mind-Body Solution
    (Quantum Publications, Inc.)
Chronic Fatigue: The Complete Mind-Body Solution
    (Quantum Publications, Inc.)
Gitanjali: Offerings from the Heart (Sound Horizons)
Growing Younger (Audio-Video Program) (Time-Life)

Video Cassettes:

The Healing Mind – Ancient Wisdom, Modern Insights
    (Quantum Publications, Inc.)
Waking Up the Power Within – The Freedom to Heal
    (Quantum Publications, Inc.)

If you would like information on workshops, lectures,
or other programs by Deepak Chopra, or to order any
of the books and tapes listed above, please contact:

Quantum Publications, Inc.
P.O. Box 598
South Lancaster, MA 01561
(800) 858-1808

The *Seven Spiritual Laws of Success* form the essence of *Creating Affluence: Wealth Consciousness in the Field of all Possibilities*. In this remarkable book, Deepak Chopra explores the full meaning of wealth consciousness and presents a series of simple A-to-Z steps and everyday actions that spontaneously generate wealth in all its forms.

Creating Affluence is available in a beautiful hardcover gift edition. This keepsake volume is a life-long companion, destined to be read and referred to again and again.

Also Available in Audio Cassette from Amber-Allen / New World Library:

The Seven Spiritual Laws of Success
Creating Affluence: Wealth Consciousness in the Field of All Possibilities

GLOBAL NETWORK FOR SPIRITUAL SUCCESS
POST OFFICE BOX 1001
DEL MAR, CALIFORNIA 92014

Dear Friend:

In *The Seven Spiritual Laws of Success*, I describe the virtues and associated principles that have helped me and countless others to achieve spiritual satisfaction and material success. I am writing to invite you to join me, and potentially millions of others worldwide, in the **Global Network for Spiritual Success**, which will be based on the daily practice of these powerful guiding principles.

Participation in the Network is open to anyone who chooses to practice The Seven Spiritual Laws. I have found it particularly fulfilling to concentrate on one law each day of the week, beginning on Sunday with the *Law of Pure Potentiality* and concluding on Saturday with the *Law of Dharma*. Having your attention on a spiritual law will completely transform your life, as it has mine, and if we collectively put our attention on the same law each day, we could soon reach a critical mass of successful people that could transform life on planet earth.

Groups of friends across the world have already begun to focus on one law each day. As I have done with my staff and friends, I suggest starting a study group of family, friends, or co-workers where members meet once a week to discuss their experiences with the spiritual laws. If the experiences are dramatic, which at times they will be, I invite you to write them down and mail them to me.

To join the **Global Network for Spiritual Success**, all you need to do is send in your name, address and, if you like, phone number and/or E-mail address to the post office box above, and we will send you a wallet-size card with the seven laws and keep you informed as the Network develops.

The establishment of the Network represents the fulfillment of one of my most cherished dreams. By joining the Global Network and practicing The Seven Spiritual Laws, I know that you will achieve spiritual success and the fulfillment of your desires. I can wish you no greater blessing.

With love and best wishes,

Deepak Chopra

Amber-Allen Publishing and New World Library
are dedicated to publishing books and cassettes that
help improve the quality of our lives. For a catalog
of our fine books and tapes, contact:

Amber-Allen / New World Library
58 Paul Drive
San Rafael, California 94903

Phone: (415) 472-2100
Fax: (415) 472-6131
Or call toll free:
(800) 227-3900